There Is Space For You.

And Other Truths

J. R. Y. Dagen

BookLeaf Publishing

India | USA | UK

Made with ❤ on the BookLeaf Publishing Platform
www.bookleafpub.in
www.bookleafpub.com

Dedication

To all those who felt there was never space for you, your story, your heart, your complexities, and your life.

To my inner child: I will take care of you.

Preface

Life is hard.

But we are resilient.

And there is space for you.

These poems are a self-exploration into all of the reasons I I felt there wasn't space for me, growing up. May they remind you that there is space for you.

Acknowledgements

My parents: Thank you for filling my world with books, and in turn, a love of writing. Thank you my safe childhood, and your faithful walks in the Lord; what an inheritance.

My love: As iron sharpens iron, you sharpen me. Thank you for keeping my feet on the ground, and helping me find the tools to build the weapons to fight for my dreams, your dreams, and our dreams. Life with you is good. I love you, dude.

Space

Space
S P A C E

It's the

    Expanse between my arms and my body

The

    Volume of myself in my chair

The

    Closeness of myself to another

The

    Cavern of my heart

The

    Labyrinth of my mind

It's

    The viscous green of not being included
    The prickly, acidic, hot feeling of being excluded.

It's

    "Your belly is so big"

And

    "Your eyes are stunning;

        You're so pretty."

It's

"I was your Secret Santa,
But since we're always together,
I kinda wish I had someone else."
And

"I heard you wanted to learn to knit,
So I bought you some needles."

It's

"Why are you so dumb?"
And

"My wife is really intelligent."

It's

"Why you? It's not like you could
Make us do anything anyway."
And

"I just wanted to call and thank you –
You make my job easy."

It's

"Why are you making this such a big deal?
Ugh, now the night is ruined."
And

"I hear what you're saying,
I'm sorry I misunderstood."

It's

    "It's not my job to defend you."

And

    "I choose you."

It's

    Conversations getting quiet when I walk in

And

    "Here; I'll scooch over for you – sit next to me."

It's

    "You're always talking about that show;

      No one wants to hear about it."

And

    "Tell me about the book you're reading."

It's

    "I won't let you leave until you kiss me."

And

    "We can stop; I don't want you to get hurt."

It's

    Setting boundaries

    Standing up for yourself

    Saying no

      And losing friends

Space
       Is growing up
                 And realizing some spaces
                 And places
          Just weren't made for you
                 No matter how you try.

Anxiety: Am I enough?. 1

Spinning,
Spinning,
A carousal of could have
                    Should have
                    Would have
            Will, won't, did.
Up and down,
            Down and up,
Questions louder than the
            Space in my head.

Plink, plink -- the xylophone
            Did I say the right thing?
Puff, puff -- the calliope,
Did I look them in the eye?
Rattle, rattle -- the snare drum.
        Too much?
                    Not enough?

Was I foolish?
Was I arrogant?
Did I talk too much?
            Too little?

Was I boastful?

Do I like them?
          Do I want to like them?
Do they like me?
          Do I want them to?

One, two, three
One, two three.
Round and round,
Up, down,
Down, up.

Am I clingy?
          Needy?
Codependent?
          Dramatic?
          Too much?
Am I understood?
Do they understand?
     Do they want to understand me?
Am I okay if they don't?

Am I welcome here?

I am not aloof.
          This trapped bird in my chest

This thick humid air
This anchor in my core
Sets brick by brick a wall.
I keep you at a distance,
I get off the ride.

Safety is not a guaranteed net --
People can be dangerous things.
Isolate.
Isolate.
Isolate.
-- Internal, I am the safest
Place to be.

Shush, child.
You are no bird.
No net ensnares you.
Breathe out.

I will be with you.
And you are enough for me.

2

Just because I am

      First

      Doesn't mean I want

      To be

        Best.

The pressure,

The pounding, unrelenting waves

    The riptide

      Pulling me towards

Perfect.

    But I don't want to be

Perfect

    Just because I have the ability to be.

    Why did it feel,

      That if I didn't achieve

        And succeed

      That I disappointed?

    Why did it feel

I couldn't just *be?*

    My procrastination,

My dragged feet,
My crossed fingers,
This was my rebellion.

How treacherous the pressure
We perceive.
I *want* to please,
To make proud –
But at what costs?
What battlelines:
Please me
Or
Please those that love me.

Carving out a life for me with a double-edged
sword,
And disappointing
Letting down,
Failing,
Hurting
Those that want the best.

The little voice
So deep in my head
It's almost my heart:
"Keep this up, you imperfect
Daughter –

You keep breaking your
		Family's heart."

I *want* to please,
		To make proud
		-- but that insipid
				Insignificant little voice
	Lieafterlieafterlieafterlie after lie after lie a f t e r l i
e a f t e r l l i i e e.

Why has it taken me
		28 years
			To give myself
				Permission
						To do the things
									I've always wanted
										To do?

Because.

I needed to release
		Myself
From internalized
		Unspoken
				Expectations.

I needed to learn that

Love
Is not

    Contingent.

3

I've always been called
"mature" –
    But am I?

    "You're so mature for your age" –
        But was I?

    Or did I internalize the identity
        Of "the bigger person'?

    Or was I afraid of disappointing
        Those that had expectations of me?

    Or did I feel the need to please
        As deep as the need to breathe?

    Or did I feel "the first"
        Through to my bones?

    Was it, perhaps,
        A challenge to this identity
        When I made
            "uncharacteristic" decisions
        When I did

           "uncharacteristic" things
     When I acted
           "uncharacteristically"?
   Under whose characterization
     Did I operate –
       That of others
         Or, myself, truly?

  Is this who I am,
     Or did I ever have
        The chance to
choose?

Health: My body, my fight. 1

I've always felt big
But today,
I actually am.
Today, I take up
The space
I was afraid I did
When I was younger.
"You're so fat."
Followed by giggles
Led me to judging myself
Against my classmates,
My peers
And feeling the wretched
Shame
When I perceived I
Was the largest in the room.

Pointing out
Someone's size
Is
Pointing out that
The sky is blue
That traffic sucks
That rain is wet

That two and two
Is four.
You,
With the pointing finger,
Clearly lack the ability
To understand
What is obvious
And what is not.
Do you think I am not
Aware
Of the size of my body?
Or is your intention
To hurt?
Because that says more about you
Than the shape of my body
Does about me.

2

Hot sweat
Drip
>Drip
>>Drip
>>Down my face
>>>My back
>>>Into my eyes.

>>How powerful
>>>Strong
>>>Capable
>>>>My body is.

Why don't I do this more often?

>My pulse,
>>Heightened
>>Excited
>My breathing
>>Deep
>>Warm
>>Raspy

I love this feeling,

Why don't I do this
          More often?

"Because", says the small, cruel voice
      "You are the fat kid,
            And have always been
the fat kid –
      Who are you if you aren't
                  Fat anymore?"

3

There is no
    Rage
    Equal to the shadow
    Left by
        Medical gaslighting.

There is no
      Despair
    Equal to climbing
    The healing mountain
        From bad medical practice
        From diagnoses given too quickly
        From doctors who didn't listen
        From providers who snipped the leaves
            But didn't pull the roots
                From weight gained

from preventable issues
                    Had someone just
listened.

And now,
    My body carries weight
        A physical sign

That I can't take care of myself
    When in reality
            I hadn't been taken care of
By those tasked with "do no harm".

This.
This is feminine rage.

4

This body of mine
What a vessel for life.
      With each year you change –
        Will you ever look the way I want?

Why do you need to die
         To decay?
          I feel too young for these grey
hairs
            Too young to see my
eyesight decline
              Too young for these
pains

This is just temporary,
      This I know.
        But change is hard,
          And this sadness is heavier
           Then I had
thought.

I feel too young
      To feel my own decline
        My own mortality.

Oh my body,
    I am learning how to take care of you
        As I know you have taken care of me
           The best you can.
              And I will fight you,
                The best I can.

Grief: The constant shadow.

1

To my grief:

You came like motion sickness
Racking my whole body
And making it hard to see
The tunnel vision,
The selfish perspectives,
The need for safety and stability –
    You turned me inside out.

I want to be angry with you,
    You intruder.
You invaded my peace of mind
And sense of emotional control.

I want to throw things at you.
Yell at you.
Pummel you.
I want to throw you out,
And pretend nothing happened.
    That you don't exist.

But how can I?

You are a gentle friend,
The grey cloak of tragic wisdom
Draped around my shoulders.
You are the soft mist of breath
That whispers in my ear
    That I do not walk alone.
You are the twin I see in the mirror,
    Forever altered.

You are the good of tragedy,
And through you,
I become human again –
    You paid the ransom
    For the kidnapped pieces of my heart.
You are the softener of tragic blows.

You have taught me gentleness
    With myself,
    With others.
You have taught me that you create Holy places
    And tender spaces
        For fellowship.
You have taught me that you open doors
    For sacrificial and
    "let me take care of you"
        Kinds of love.

You have taught me the capacity I have for love,
And how far I can dissolve
And still come back together.
You have taught me that your daughter is joy
And your granddaughter is thankfulness
And like the Fates,
You move together.

You are forever a part of me.
In the tone of my voice.
The look in my eyes.
The frame of my shoulders.
The depth of my laugh.
The sounds of my footsteps.
You've matured me,
And my glasses are no longer rosy.

How can I be angry with you,
When you've led me into places of shared grief?

You are a part of me, Grief;
I feel you peeking through the shutters to read this.
You arrived with a sob so loud
I thought it was me,
But now, I hear you whisper
Only when you're called.

You have ping-balled me into unfamiliar
    Unknown territory,
        But with you as my guide
            I know I will come out the other
side.

To my grief,
    You are a part of me –
    I know we will meet again,
        Though I ask,
            Please,
                Not for a long time.

2

I am self-conscious
        Of my grief.
        Is it too
                        Obvious
                In the depths of my eyes?
                In the lines of my face?
                In the shape of my shoulders?
                In the sound of my laugh?
                In the talk of my future?
                        In discussions of my health?

Does is billow
        Behind me
                A heavy cloak
                        Of soft shadows?

Do I give it away
        When I'm asked
                "Do you have any kids?"
                Do I take too long
                        Before I deflect?

I have children
        I will never

Know –
I have children
That will never know me
Or their father,
Until we are called Home –

What an awful emptiness.

This –
This breaking and re-stitching
Of my tender, hopeful heart –
Is a part of the
Very fabric
Of who I am
Now.

I am self-conscious of my grief.

The tidal wave
Has left me
Treading water,
Not in hope
But in reservation
In hesitation
In fear
In reality.

I am self-conscious
    Self aware
Of the foolishness
    Of clinging to
            Hope
For something
    I am not
    Promised.

But how do you
    Release
        The deepest
Desire of your heart?

This,
    I do not know.

This is not
    "a personality trait"
I have known Death
    The gripping pains of wretched intimacy –
I have been drowned
    In the life-altering
            Tsunami
    Of futures that
            Could have,

But won't be.

I am self-conscious
    Of my grief.
Time rubs away
    The sharpness
    The community
    The support –
How do you ask to
Not be forgotten
    When it was never
        Theirs to carry?

How can I ask
    For my babies
        To be remembered?

This broken mother's heart
    Is terrified
        That being forgotten
            Means
                That my babies
                    Did not matter
                    At all.

3

Grief is a funny thing.

It throws you under water
    Then shows you
        How to breathe.

It slaps you in the face,
    Then kisses your cheek.

It lights your feathers on fire
    Until you dissolve into
        A pile of soot,
Then whispers in your ashy ears
        "Rise."

Grief exerts its authority
    All consuming
        And all powerful
    It tells you there is no escape,
        Then helps you find a door.

It is contrasts and impossibles –
    How can something
        So vicious

Become so soft?

Grief is a funny thing –
　　It lays in wait to pounce,
　　　　But then stands in the shadows
　　　　　Ready to embrace.

A cousin of the Reaper,
　　Grief knows us all by name,
　　　　But it's seven faces
　　　　　Are not all the same.

My grief,
　　It is a funny, almost forgotten,
　　　　Just as heavy
　　　　Just as tender
　　　　Still as uninvited
　　　　　　Thing.

4

Please don't let me stay
In the place
      I forget Your Name.
For You are Good,
      You have been Good
         You will be Good,
            For it's Your Name.

Others: My place, their space. 1

I have felt like
Oil
  To others'
    Water.

My interest
  Skills
   Pursuits
   Goals
    Dreams
   Weren't theirs.

My humor
  Wasn't theirs.

What brought me
  Joy
   Laughter
   Fun
    Wasn't theirs.

We were two
  Opposing magnets –

Bumping and sliding apart

Do I overlook
   The central parts
      Of who I am
         To make friends
                  Memories
         Be included --
Or
      Do I hold fast
         To *me*
         And wade through
      the murky waters
         to find common ground?

How deeply problematic
   To so deeply
      Want to relate
         And feel the
         Odd
                  One
                  Out.

2

It's taken a lot of time –
    A lot of loneliness
        To learn I am not
           Entitled
        To friendships.

        I am not entitled
                To be liked.

        I am not entitled
           To be sought out –
                If I'm not willing
                    To do so too.

It's taken me a lot of time
      To learn
        That this is a two way street
           And those that choose me
           Walk with me
              When I ask them to.

I am worthy of being liked
      But I won't fit into everyone's puzzle.
And it's taken me

A lot of time
    And loneliness
To learn that rejection
    Does not
        Always
          Mean
            That I am less than
            That I am not worthy
            That I am unlikeable
            That I am too much
            It just means the fit wasn't right.

Some drink coffee,
    And I'm a cup of tea.
Some drink wine,
    And I'm Henny straight.
Some are oil
    And I am water.

It's taken me a lot of time
    And loneliness –
        To learn that what I bring
        Is not needed
            Or wanted
At every table.

3

It was a liar
Who said
That healing was straight --
It's not even up and down.

It's a looping
  Rollercoaster,
  A never-ending circle;
  A chaotic,
  Noisy
  Pin-ball machine.

There's reminders all over
  Wedding photos
  Shared friends
  Names murmured
  Afraid to offend.
  Wounds re-picked.

This would just be easier
  If there was a gravestone,
  But I see you at church
  Hear your name among friends
  See you online

And then I need to start all over.

Healing is untying a necklace
that got jumbled in your pocket
 and it keeps knotting up again.

Healing is annoying
and frustrating --
                but I guess I should be made of sterner
stuff
                by now.

4

My dear,
  My love,
    My man.

By these flowers you have bought me
    Just today,
      On this table
        That we've had
          In this life
            We are building;
              Here I sit.

You have wrecked beautiful havoc
    On my patterns of love
      You've smoothed over my
        Fears
        Anxieties
          And taken my needs
          In stride.

Life is sweet
  And you are good.
And in these quiet night sounds

There is no place I would rather
Be.

Myself: I like me today. 1

My heart
>Is tender and soft –
>>Would you believe
>>>It
>>>If you met me?

Would you believe
>My heart spent years
>>Paralyzed by
>>>Glances
>>>>Facial expressions
>>>>Tones of voice
>>>>Body language
>>>>Words?

My heart is so soft
>It built
>>A moat of sass
>>A wall of snark
>>>Hired a guard of humor
>>And buried deep
>>>Deep
>>>>Down
>Locked in the treasure room

Lies my soft and weary heart.

My gentle heart
        Is not easily fooled.
She has no more patience
            For words that
                Don't match
                    Your eyes
            For actions that
                Don't match
                    Your words
            For words that
                Don't match
                    Your actions

She has, too many times,
    Offered herself
        With wiling open arms
    To only be destroyed
        By those who
            Did not see
                Her glass skin.

But yet.
    Again and again,
        She tries.

My heart self-sabotages –
    She gives her self so easily,
        To only,
            Too late,
Question if she was
    Ever wanted in the first place.

My heart is self-conscious –
    She is torn between taking care of
        And protecting herself
            And not hurting the hearts of others.

My heart is afraid –
    She has hurt
        So many people
            Because she said the wrong words
            Because she offered what she couldn't
deliver
            Because she said "yes" when she
wanted to say "no.

She has hurt herself
        Because she didn't say "no"
        Because she didn't say "stop" –
            Because she valued others' hearts
above her own.

My heart is *sensitive* –
	She feels the world
		In all its complexities
			And intensities
		And it fills her
			From the top of her head
			To the tips of her toes
				And out her eyes.

The key to the treasure room is hidden
	Because she's been called dramatic too many
times
	Because she's felt her tenderness is an
inconvenience
	Because she's been walked over,
		Talked over,
			Talked about.

This world is too harsh
	For a heart
		That feels the news
			As a smack in the face.

This world is too heavy
	For a heart
		That is just now
			Secure enough

To learn
That disagreements
Do not need to mean
An end.

This world is too heavy
For a heart
That is just now
Learning
That the right people –
The best kind of people –
Create the space
For her to just be.

In her imprisonment,
My heart has split in two;
Her tough twin now rules.

This twin
Walks in confidence
Speaks in grace
Governs in diplomacy
Operates in fairness
Breathes through criticisms
Releases disagreements
Laughs at
Is no longer crippled by

Rudeness.

There are still times
    When she hides
        Behind her soft sister,
            And when she does,
                The kingdom shakes.

My soft heart,
    My tender heart,
        She has begun to look
            for the
                    key.
She is making known
    She is still here
        Inside my chest
            Barely beating,
But no need to worry,
    She is stretching
                    for the
                            sun.

2

I've hardly taken the time
>To pause
>and see
>>The miles that I've come
>>The heights that I've climbed
>Why is it so hard to be proud of me?

I've done things
>My little heart
>>Always dreamed
>And have found
>>New dreams
>>>Along the way.

My dreams aren't drifting balloons
>Floating just out of reach –
>>They never were, really,
>>>I just didn't know
>>>>They were for me.

Why is it so hard to be proud of me?

See, I am capable
>Of big things –

This, I've seen;
    And there is a difference
        Between pride and arrogance.

Why do I underplay
    My joy in what I've done?
Didn't I know that it's infectious,
    And is spread
        One
            By
                One?

If I'm honest,
    And I should be,
        I am proud of me.

3

Oh little heart,
    You've grown up.

You've taken on new titles
    New roles
      New responsibilities.

The world is on your shoulders
    Now
    Instead of for the taking.

Oh little heart,
    Why has the magic faded?

Why were you so
    Eager
     To be
  "a big girl now"? –
     To see the world
      Behind all its curtains
        To take off the rosy glasses?

The world is much
    More vast

And complicated
And different
And beautiful
And harsh
And intimate
And wonderful
And not like you imagined.

Oh little heart,
I am sorry for the pain
You carry –
Harsh words from people you trusted
Insensitive hands which didn't hold
Your outstretched heart
Deep wounds from hurts you've
caused
Deep grief from what's been taken

The world is an unfeeling dealer;
I am sorry this is your hand.

But little heart,
Nestled deep inside,
Your little hand in mind,
Your little eyes in mine,
I will take care of you.

I will take care of you.

Walk in my footsteps,
     Rest in my shadows –
          I see you fully.

I am a safe place,
     And I will take care of you.

4

I like me today.
    I care about me
        Today.

I am my own
    Nice warm cuppa
    Double shot of whiskey
        Best friend
            Today.

Me
  Myself
     And I
       Have had many
        Versions
        Seasons
        Chapters
          And I like
           This one
        The best.

Space.

Space.

S P A C E

    There is no part of you

        That is so unknown

            That you are forever lost.

                In this

world

                In this

life

  There is space

    For you.